GW00601066

To...........

From....................

Purple Ronnie's
Little Book for
The World's Best
M ♥ U ♥ M

by Purple Ronnie

First published 2009 by Boxtree
an imprint of Pan Macmillan Ltd
Pan Macmillan, 20 New Wharf Road, London N1 9RR
Basingstoke and Oxford
Associated companies throughout the world
www.panmacmillan.com

ISBN 978-0-7522-2698-9

Copyright © Purple Enterprises Ltd, a Coolabi company 2009

All rights reserved. No part of this publication may be
reproduced, stored in or introduced into a retrieval system, or
transmitted, in any form, or by any means (electronic, mechanical,
photocopying, recording or otherwise) without the prior written
permission of the publisher. Any person who does any unauthorized
act in relation to this publication may be liable to criminal
prosecution and civil claims for damages.

9 8 7 6 5 4 3 2 1

A CIP catalogue record for this book is
available from the British Library.

Printed and bound in Hong Kong

'Purple Ronnie' created by Giles Andreae. The right of Giles Andreae and Janet Cronin
to be identified respectively as the author and illustrator of this work has been asserted by them
in accordance with the Copyright, Designs and Patents Act 1988.

Visit **www.panmacmillan.com** to read more about all our books
and to buy them. You will also find features, author interviews and
news of any author events, and you can sign up for e-newsletters
so that you're always first to hear about our new releases.

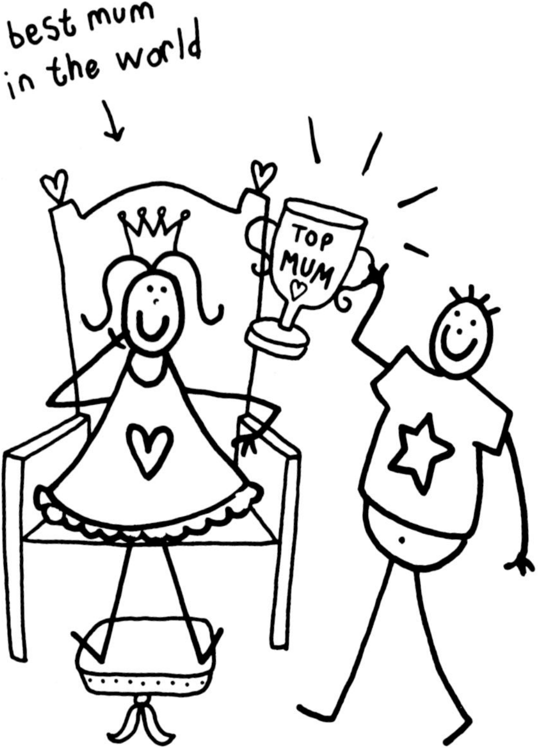
best mum
in the world
TOP
MUM

a poem for ↓

My Mum

Being a mum is a difficult
job

That's not always easy
to do

But if I could choose the
best Mum in the world

I know I would go and
pick you

Warning:-

No-one can embarrass you as brilliantly as a Mum can

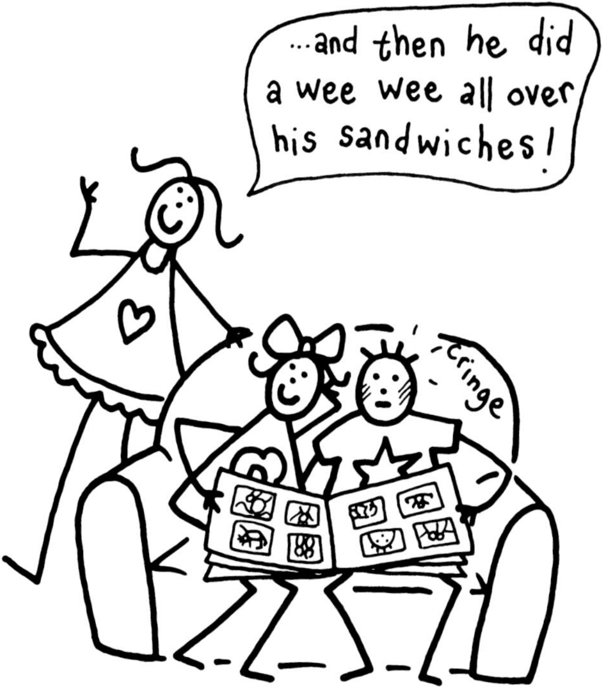
...and then he did a wee wee all over his sandwiches!
cringe

Cuddles

The brilliant thing about
a mum
Is when you're in a muddle
She can always make it
better
Just by giving you a cuddle!

Remember:-

Sometimes even Mums need a little bit of spoiling

a poem for a

Lovely Mum

Mums can be embarrassing

And Mums can be a bore

But you're a really fab
one

And I couldn't love you
more

Mums and their Bodies

Some Mums get completely obsessed by keeping fit. Others don't mind at all being a bit wobbly

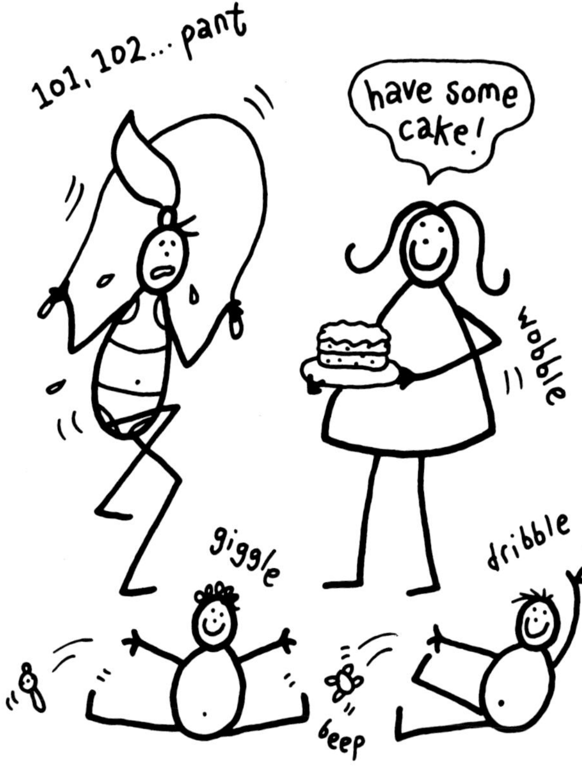
101, 102... pant
have some cake!
wobble
giggle
dribble
beep

Your Mum

No matter how successful

Or how famous you become

No matter what great
things you do

Your mum is still your
mum

Being Nice

It is always a good idea to be nice to your Mum. You never know when you might need her

SALE
natter
ooh! that's gorgeous!
NOW
SHOES
massive shopping trip

a poem for a

Brilliant Mum

Some Mums can be batty
And can drive you round
the bend
But you're not just a
brilliant one

You're also a fab friend

Some Mums can't help
being critical when
they think they are
trying to help.

You must do your best
to ignore them

Mums

It's almost unbelievable

When looking at your mum

To think a great big

lump like you

Was once inside her tum!

Remember :-

Being a Mum is one of the busiest jobs in the world. It is nice to give them a bit of help from time to time

brrr

you chilling out

a poem for

My Fab Mum

Why don't you put your
feet up
And take the day off too

Cos it must be very
hard to be

A Mum as fab as you

The biggest treat a
Mum can have is to
know that her little
darlings are happy

Soppy Mums

There's nothing like a soppy
film
Or drama on the telly
To make a mum get weepy
And tremble like a jelly!

Mums and Driving

Even the most patient Mum can turn into a complete maniac when she gets behind a steering wheel

a poem for my
Groovy Mum

I wrote you this poem
to tell you

You're groovy, you're fab
and you're fun

And I really just wanted
to thank you

For being a wonderful mum

Beware

Mums are absolute experts at giving annoying advice

Mums' Presents

The strangest thing about
some mums
Is how they really hope
That when they get a
present
It'll just be scented soap !

keeping in Touch

If you are miles away from home, even the shortest phone call can make your Mum unbelievably happy

a poem for a

Star Mum

Has anyone recently told
you

How totally smashing
you are

If not here's a poem to
tell you

That this person thinks
you're a star

Mother's Day

Make sure you remember
(It can't be all that hard)
That when it comes to
Mother's Day
You MUST give her a card!

Special Tip

Mums love nothing
more than a lovely
bunch of flowers

a poem for a
Magic Mum

Here's a little message

For a Mum who is the tops

It's to tell you that you're
magic

And to say I love you
lots

The great thing about Mums is that they're always there when you need them

I got chucked!
there there, never mind, plenty more fish in the sea etc. etc
boo-hoo
sob
YOU'RE CHUCKED

My Fab Mum

I want to say how fab you are

And here's the reason why

You're always there to cheer me up

Well, you and chocolate pie!

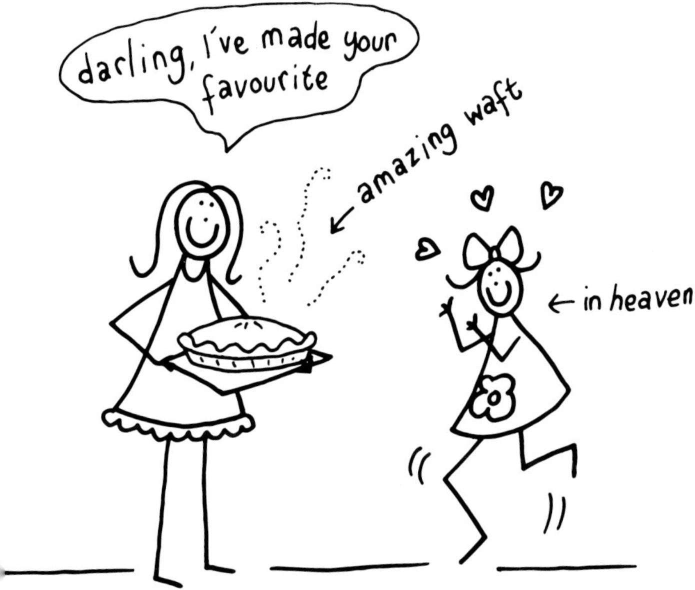
darling, I've made your favourite
amazing waft
in heaven

Warning:—
Some mums just don't
realise that we <u>change</u>
as we get older

Look, dear, your favourite-
raspberry jelly!
beam
wobble
but that was
when I was five

a poem for a
↓
Marvellous Mum

I know that it sounds
cheesy
But I'm telling you it's true
It's fab to have a Mum
who is as marvellous
as you

Some Mums never stop thinking that you're still their little baby